Because
of
Her

AMANDA SCHNABLE

ISBN 978-1-64492-679-6 (paperback)
ISBN 978-1-64492-680-2 (digital)

Christian Faith Publishing, Inc.
832 Park Avenue
Meadville, PA 16335
www.christianfaithpublishing.com

Printed in the United States of America

Carve your name on hearts, not tombstones.
A legacy is etched into the
minds and hearts of others
and the stories they share about you.

—Author Shannon Alder

To my mother, Linda.

Contents

Acknowledgments

I would like to thank my grandparents, Vernon and Grace, for their incredible spirit of caring and giving. When life threw you a curveball and brought your daughter and two grandchildren back to live with you, you gave us all the much-needed support, love, and guidance we needed to keep going.

To my wonderful Aunt Karen, thank you for the countless hours of babysitting, sleepovers, and support, helping me become the woman I am today. The annual birthday-shopping outings will never be forgotten! You will always hold a special place in my heart.

To my older sister, Lisa, I am so thankful and blessed to have you in my life. We have walked the same long hard road of overwhelming circumstances together, and I can't think of a better person to have had along my side growing up. The love I have in my heart for you is colossal. The bond between sisters can never be broken.

To my three sons, you are the reason I strive to be a better person. There is nothing greater than the blessing of children, and I am honored to be your mom. You each hold a special place in my heart and were given to me by God at just the right time.

To my husband, Bryan, thank you for your never-ending love and support. At the end of the day, you're still the one my heart longs for.

Introduction

This story is based on actual true events from my mother's life. From the time she was twenty-four years old until she was forty-three years young, she fought a reoccurring brain tumor. Undergoing twenty various brain surgeries and treatments within a fifteen-year time span, she beat the odds of fighting a tumor that without the hand and favor of an Almighty God, could have never been accomplished by medical professionals alone. She was one of the bravest women I have ever known. All who knew her would say the same thing. She never complained, never gave up, always had a good attitude, and always believed that God was working out all things together for her good.

Through all of her hardships and health challenges, she always had a smile on her face. Her faith and love in the Lord have encouraged me and many others over the years and continues to inspire me even after her passing.

I share this amazing true story with you so that you will see God's faithfulness in every situation, even in the bad ones. I look forward to the day I get to see her again face-to-face in heaven. Until then, I hope that this story will encourage women of all ages that no matter what your circumstances may be, God is always with you, fighting your battles, and working all things together for your good.

*"The Lord will fight for you, you
need only to be still"* (Exodus 14:14, NIV).

Chapter 1

A Beautiful New Beginning

There is a time for everything, and a sea-
son for every activity under the heavens.
—Ecclesiastes 3:1 (NIV)

It was a warm, sunny day in June as I slipped into my white wedding dress. Today would be the day I would walk down the aisle and marry my high school sweetheart. John was a star football player, handsome, and very well-liked in school. All the girls had their eye on him, and I know they were jealous when he picked me to be his sweetheart. My dream of becoming a wife to this handsome young man, who had stolen my heart, was becoming a reality in our little town that day. In just a few short hours, we would be husband and wife and start our life together.

The wedding was everything I had hoped it would be. The minister blessed us, the kiss was fantastic, and the walk down the aisle as mister and misses felt amazing. I had my whole life in front of me, and I couldn't wait to spend it with John.

After the ceremony and reception, we found our vehicle parked outside of the church. The words *Just Married* had been artistically applied to the windows with white shoe polish while aluminum cans had been fastened to the back bumper with the use of strings. It was just how I had imagined it would be as we pulled out of the church parking lot that warm summer day. As we listened to the clanking of the cans on the pavement behind us, we kissed each other lovingly and waved goodbye to our friends and family. Peace and joy filled our hearts as we drove away to our honeymoon destination. I couldn't wait to begin our life together as husband and wife.

"To have and to hold from this day forward—for better, for worse; for richer, for poorer; in sickness and in health, to love and to cherish, till death us do part." Those were the vows we recited at our ceremony. We were young and in love. Little did we know, the hard times ahead that would put those very words to test.

Loving John was easy. He was handsome, strong, funny, and a very hard worker. I knew with all my heart he would be my sweetheart forever. It wasn't long after the wedding that we quickly found ourselves in a regular routine of working nine-to-five. John worked for a trucking company and primarily drove a dump truck and hauled sand and gravel for a living. I worked as a cashier at a local department store. Within a very short time, I found out we were expecting our first child, a baby girl.

How exciting! I thought. Me, a mother. This was something I've always wanted. I remembered writing a short story in my junior year of high school about what I wanted to do after school. I wanted to get married, be a homemaker, and be a mother who stayed home with her kids. And now it was happening!

John and I made the decision that I would leave my job after the baby came. Nevertheless, I continued to work right up until the time our daughter was born. I was so proud of John for working so hard to provide for our family, so I could enjoy staying at home with our daughter.

Time passed and I absolutely loved being at home. I would get up early each morning to make John a bacon-and-egg-breakfast sandwich and see him off to work. I would then spend the rest of the day taking care of our home, preparing the meals for the week, and spending quality time with our little one. I was so thankful for the wonderful life we shared. We excitedly looked forward to trying to have more children in the future.

Being a homemaker and taking care of our daughter was everything I dreamed of. I loved being a wife—cooking, baking, and making our home a place of peace and rest. Life was so enjoyable. While our budget was tight on one income, we did everything possible to make things work so that I could stay home.

After a hard day's work, John would return home, and I was always excited for him to be with us in the evening. I was starting to dream about the right time to have another baby to complete our family. I didn't want a super large family, just one (maybe two) more children. John and I excitedly looked forward to our future.

Chapter 2

Seizures and Epilepsy

The righteous person may have many troubles,
but the Lord delivers him from them all.
—Psalm 34:19, NIV

A new year had started, and we had just celebrated my twenty-fourth birthday. Our little girl was now two years old. My birthday was on December 2, and I can remember always wanting a little sister when I was younger. You can imagine my excitement when my mother told me she was expecting a baby when I was eight years old. I truly thought I would burst.

Then on December 2, the day of my ninth birthday, my mother gave birth to my baby sister, Karen Sue. Not only did I have a baby sister now like I had always wanted, but we also shared the same birthday! My excitement faded just a little bit though on the day my parents brought her home.

"She's too little to play with me. When will she be able to play?" I asked.

Little did I know at the time, but this little sister God brought home to me would turn out to be one of my greatest blessings ever in my future.

Every morning, I woke up with John to prepare his favorite breakfast sandwich, which consisted of one fried egg and three slices of bacon, sandwiched in between two pieces of buttered toast. One morning while standing over the stove preparing breakfast, I noticed I wasn't feeling well. I wasn't quite sure what was going on. I began to feel a sense of trembling in my entire body. I broke out in a cold sweat, and a metallic taste developed in my mouth. I then became short-winded. I went from feeling warm and sweating to feeling very cold with a sense of frigid wind blowing over me. Then I went back to sweating. I walked to the bathroom to splash water on my face to see if it would help.

While standing at the bathroom sink, trying to get the water turned on, everything faded and went black. The next thing I remembered was my sweet husband holding me in his lap, stroking my hair, and holding a damp, cool washcloth over my forehead.

"Are you alright?" John asked with concern. "Wake up, please wake up." When he had been in the kitchen earlier, he had heard a loud thump from the bathroom and came running in to check on me. He found me lying on the bathroom floor. The thump he heard was my body hitting the tub. I had no recollection of what had happened to me.

My body was not my own. It was as if something had completely taken over my ability to function. I couldn't think clearly and felt confused. I desperately wanted to tell him I was okay and not to worry, but my mouth couldn't speak what I wanted to say. I felt very disoriented and wondered if I was just overly tired? Neither one of us could make sense of what exactly was happening or why I fell over in the bathroom that morning. We both thought it was a fluke happening, and I just fainted for some unknown reason. I promised John if it happened again anytime soon, I would go to the doctor. We tried not to worry about it and went on with our day.

Days and months went on, and I continued to dream of having another baby to complete our family and give our little girl a sibling. About six months later, while making breakfast and helping John get ready and off to work, this same feeling came over me again and came on quicker than the last time. I didn't have time to walk to the bathroom or the couch this time. I dropped to the floor right there on the cold tile in the kitchen, and this time my whole body started shaking. John did everything he could to try and help me and control my jerking and involuntary movements. After the shaking stopped, and I was back to my normal self, I asked John, "What is happening to me? Why is this happening to my body?"

"I don't know, sweetheart, but we have to find out."

This second episode really shook both of us to our core.

We made a doctor's appointment immediately to get me thoroughly checked out. After several different exams and tests, the doctor diagnosed me as having epilepsy. Epilepsy is a disorder in which nerve cell activity in the brain is disturbed, causing seizures. What had happened to me those two mornings at home was a seizure. He sent me home with two different seizure medications to try and control them and hopefully prevent them from happening at all.

After a month of taking these new medications, the seizures continued to happen. Every time an episode occurred, the jerking and shaking got more intense. I was grateful and thankful that a seizure never occurred when I was alone with our young daughter. John or my mother was always with me when one occurred. This was a huge blessing for me because I always feared having one while I was alone with her. Over the next few months in addition to the seizures, I started to develop headaches along with some blurry and double vision.

My doctor performed a CT Scan of my brain, and they discovered some edema. Edema is also known as brain swelling. It causes fluid to develop in the brain. This fluid increases the pressure inside of the skull, which was why I was now experiencing headaches and vision problems. The doctor never wanted to do anything about the edema, he just wanted to watch it and wanted me to continue on my prescription medications.

John and my parents were not happy with us just watching the edema on the brain, and they hoped I would seek out another opinion. However, I liked the doctor I was going to, and I was hoping the medications he gave me along with prayer would be all I would need to get me through this.

Chapter 3

A Miracle Baby

*For you created my inmost being; you knit me
together in my mother's womb. I praise you because
I am fearfully and wonderfully made; your works
are wonderful, I know that full well. My frame
was not hidden from you when I was made in
the secret place, when I was woven together in the
depths of the earth. Your eyes saw my unformed
body, all the days ordained for me were written
in your book before one of them came to be.*
—Psalm 139:13–16 (NIV)

At the end of an examination, after discussing the plan for medications to control the seizures and recently discovered edema, the doctor wanted to speak to me about something that was very serious. He asked me to absolutely not consider having any more children in my future with my medical condition. The medications I was taking were far too dangerous for a baby in the womb during pregnancy. My epileptic condition could provoke dangerous seizures during labor and delivery, therefore, causing harm to both myself and the baby. This was devastating news for me!

I cried all the way home in the car that day, thinking over and over why was this happening to me, to us? I cried out to God and said, "Lord, you know my desire to have another child. All I want in life is to be a homemaker, a good wife, and have children, and raise a family."

I was saddened for weeks about this. John and I talked about how serious we should be about this, and that we should not have any more children. John agreed to make an appointment to talk with his doctor about having a vasectomy done.

However, right after this conversation, just a few short weeks later, I found myself feeling extra tired and nauseous. One morning while making my routine egg-and-bacon sandwiches, the smell of the bacon frying sent me to the bathroom, thinking I was going to throw up. I stood over the toilet that morning thinking, *Great, now what is wrong with me?* All of a sudden, it hit me that I was late with my monthly menstrual cycle. Could I be pregnant? Fear and excitement ran through me all at the same time!

Later that afternoon, I took an over-the-counter pregnancy test, and it was positive! I was overcome with joy. I cried and cried some more. Then my joy turned to fear about what the doctor had told us just a few weeks prior about not having any more children. How was I going to explain this to John and the doctor? I knew they would disapprove and be upset with me for allowing this to happen. However, I couldn't shake the feeling inside my spirit that God is the one who had allowed this to happen and was giving me the desires of my heart.

"Delight yourself in the Lord, and He will give you the desires of your heart" (Psalm 37:4, ESV).

I decided right then and there that I didn't care what the medical diagnosis was for my health. I serve a big and powerful God, and he knows the desires of my heart, and he blessed me with this pregnancy, and he would see me through this. I had all trust and belief in my faith that the Lord would see me through this. Immediately, scripture verses that I had grew up with and heard all my life instantly flooded my mind.

So do not fear, for I am with you, do not be dismayed, for I am your God. I will strengthen you and help you, I will uphold you with my righteous right hand. (Isaiah 41:10, NIV)

Have I not commanded you? Be strong and courageous. Do not be afraid; do not be discouraged, for the Lord your God will be with you wherever you go. (Joshua 1:9, NIV)

I walked out of the bathroom that day with all confidence in my faith that the Lord would see me through this. We made an appointment with my doctor right away though because we did have concerns about the medications I was taking to prevent the seizures. Would they cause harm to the baby? Should I stop taking them during this first trimester? Tons of questions flooded my mind about what I should or should not be doing during this time?

The doctor was not pleased when I told him I was pregnant. So much displeased that he even encouraged me to consider terminating the pregnancy. Terminating the pregnancy never even crossed my mind, and I would not entertain that idea at all! I responded to the doctor that I was going to keep this baby growing inside of me, so he was just going to have to help me through this.

It was in my best interest to continue taking my seizure medications during the pregnancy. We all had some concerns what it might do to the baby. However I was confident that if the Lord blessed me with this baby, he would see me through. I prayed daily for good health, safety, and protection over this new blessing in my womb. Only because of God's goodness and power can I say that during the entire pregnancy I did not have one seizure.

As the end of the pregnancy was drawing near, we did have some concerns still about what labor and delivery would bring for me, and we continued to pray for safety and health over the delivery and that zero seizures would happen during that time.

On a bitterly cold and snowy weekend in December, labor pains began for me and my water broke. We ventured off to the hospital in the dangerous winter weather and prepared to meet the newest addition to our family. My heart raced with anticipation to bring another child into our lives. I was so sure that God had everything under control, and I just kept praying a prayer inside my spirit that this baby would be healthy and whole and that none of the medications I had taken would have effected this baby's health in anyway. I also held on to my faith that our prayers would sustain me through the labor and delivery and that there would be no complications for my health.

After several hours of labor on New Year's Eve morning, I delivered another beautiful baby girl. Labor and delivery went smoothly for me with no concerns or seizures of any kind. I was so grateful and thankful that the Lord was watching over me just as he had promised to me when I found out I was expecting. After thorough examinations over the baby, we were all delighted and overjoyed that the baby was as healthy as could be, and as far as we could tell this early in her life, there were no health concerns that we should be concerned with at all. I felt the Lord's presence and peace over us, and I knew all the glory and praise was due to him.

***A miracle, my miracle baby, that is what this was!
With man, they see and say impossible—but with God,
all things are possible!***

> *O Lord, you alone are my hope. I've trusted you from childhood. Yes, you have been with me from birth; from my mother's womb you have cared for me. No wonder I am always praising you! My life is an example to many, because you have been my strength and protection. That is why I can never stop praising you, I declare your glory all day long.* (Psalm 71:5–8, NIV)

Chapter 4

The Unthinkable

And the peace of God, which tran-
scends all understanding, will guard your
hearts and minds in Christ Jesus.
—Philippians 4:7, NIV

We were enjoying our two precious girls and feeling so thankful for God's blessing of children in our lives. After our second daughter was born, John went ahead with the vasectomy appointment and had the procedure done as we were confident our family was complete with our two perfect daughters. I continued to take my seizure medications to control seizure activity. However, about a year and a half after her birth, my seizures, headaches, double and blurry vision started to worsen. We decided I should go see a different doctor, a neurosurgeon who specialized in these kinds of things and get a new CT scan.

John had to work on the day of the appointment, so I left my two girls in the caring hands of my younger sister, Karen Sue, so I could go to the appointment by myself. She was now a responsible teenager, and she loved helping me with our girls.

As I waited for the doctor to share the results of the exam and new CT scan with me, I could sense that something wasn't right. At a time when I should have been extremely afraid and fearful, I had a sweet presence of peace over me, knowing that whatever the doctor told me, I would get through with the Lord's help.

The diagnosis was not good. I had a brain tumor and this was the chief reason for all my symptoms.

"Linda, we will need to schedule you for surgery to remove this brain tumor as soon as possible," the doctor reported.

"How soon?" I asked the doctor.

"In the next few days," he replied.

I had so much to think about and prepare for this brain surgery. I had two little girls at home that needed caretakers during this time. And to top it off, my parents were on a vacation in Colorado. They had just left a few days prior to this appointment, and they wouldn't be coming home for another week. I could not have brain surgery without my mom here. I just wouldn't consider it. I needed her strength, prayers, and her comfort for my two girls. I called my parents right away at the hotel where they were staying before scheduling the surgery and made them aware of this news. They were so concerned and anxious to get to us, they packed right up and drove all night from Colorado to Missouri so that they could be with me.

I left the doctor appointment with all kinds of emotions going through me. How was I going to tell John and the rest of our family? I drove around and around and around. I don't even know where I drove exactly. I eventually ended up back at my parents' home where my sister had been caring for my girls, and John was there waiting for me.

I should have been home hours ago, and he was deeply concerned why I was so late. When I walked in the kitchen, he could tell something was deeply wrong with me. When I reported the news to him, we both broke down in tears and held each other for what seemed like an eternity. I was so grateful that my sister was there to take care of the girls and distract them from this news. Her presence with the girls allowed John and I the time to talk about the upcoming surgery.

Looking back over my life, I count my sister as one of my greatest blessings because what I didn't know at the time (but know now), she was a pillar of strength in my girls' lives and would continue to be in the years ahead.

The hardest part of facing this first surgery was accepting the fact that I had to have my head shaved, and I would have to be apart from the girls for so many days. Telling our friends and family was also very traumatic as the shock was just too much for some.

The year was 1980, and this was my first brain surgery. The girls were two and six years old.

Once again, the Lord was faithful to me and carried me through this surgery. The doctor felt confident that he had removed all of the tumor and reported that I should have a smooth and relatively easy recovery. With help from physical and occupational therapy, I was back to my old self in no time and regaining my strength. We were all very thankful for the Lord's hand of blessing and favor over my life. I looked forward to the days of recovery ahead to get back to my normal life and raising our girls.

Chapter 5

The House

I will bless the Lord at all times; his praise
shall continually be in my mouth.
—Psalm 34:1 (KJV)

Shortly after my recovery, we bought a small piece of land and started building our dream house. We built this house in the same community where we both grew up. It was close to our families and just a few minutes away from our church where we attended. This was our very first home together, as we had been living in a rental duplex up until this point.

Our family and friends all pulled together alongside John to make this dream house of ours possible. John was such a hard worker, and he wanted to provide the girls and I with a lovely home. It was a ranch-style home with three bedrooms and two baths. All brick on the outside and a lovely front porch, viewing the beautiful piece of land.

The yard was what I liked the most because I could see our girls running and playing and having fun. The house was tucked away off the main road down a long gravel driveway, so I didn't have to worry about the girls playing outside. It was quiet and peaceful.

Once again, I was so thankful in the faithfulness of God for providing so many rich blessings upon me. With my choice to be a stay-at-home mother and homemaker, we definitely did not have a lot of extra money to spare. The things we did have, we could afford though, we tried very hard not to go in over our heads in too much debt. The only debt we had was the mortgage on our home. We tried not to live beyond our means. We were happy and had peace and joy in our home, which were very valuable things that money couldn't buy.

In an attempt to earn some extra spending money for myself and the girls, I did work a few hours a week outside of the home, helping a friend of the family with an elderly disabled man who needed help with housekeeping, grocery shopping, and other small tasks. I was happy to be helpful to him, and it was a way for me to earn some extra spending money, and I could take my girls along with me to help as well.

The next several years were relatively normal, healthy, and filled with fun family memories. We enjoyed camping, fishing, and riding Jeeps along the banks of the Black River in Lesterville, Missouri. We attended our local church on a regular basis, and I taught young girls on a weekly basis in a program that was called Missionettes.

Missionettes was the original name of the National Girls Ministries program of the Assemblies of God. This young-girls-mentoring program is now called National Girls Ministries Girls Club. In this weekly program, the goal was that an older woman would develop relationships with younger girls and teach them about God's word, how to serve in the church, serve others, and develop their gifts and talents along with memorizing scripture verses.

I absolutely loved teaching young girls about the love and faithfulness of the Lord and leading them into their relationship with Jesus Christ. These midweekly meetings were one of the highlights of my week. My girls were very active in this ministry as well, and I loved volunteering and seeing them succeed in this program.

I was raised in this Christian Bible-believing church where I was serving and was also involved in a weekly woman's prayer team, as well as the woman's bowling league through our church. I loved bowling, and I loved praying, so getting to do both of those things with my friends was a great treat. John played on the church's softball league. We had a lot of fun summers getting together with other families from our church, playing ball and camping along the river with them.

Life was really looking good for us, and we were thankful that the tumor had not returned and that I was not having any more seizures. I was thoroughly enjoying my life and raising our two girls was my whole world.

Five years had passed by quickly since my first brain tumor surgery, and we were all ecstatic that I had not had any more trouble or concerns.

Chapter 6

The Unexpected

From the ends of the earth I call to you,
I call as my heart grows faint; lead me
to the rock that is higher than I.
— Psalm 61:2 (NIV)

Shortly after the five-year anniversary of my first brain tumor surgery, I noticed my headaches started to return and then came the blurry and double vision again. Slowly but surely, the seizures returned as well. There were many days that my girls had to get me to a safe place in our living room and move the furniture around, so I could have my seizures without hurting myself. I would sleep for hours after a major seizure, and the girls were so loving and brave. They would get me all snuggled up on the couch with a pillow and blanket and made sure I could sleep after a major episode.

Another routine CT scan showed once again that the tumor had returned, and this time, with a vengeance. I needed another surgery. This was heartbreaking for me since five years had passed with no signs of trouble. I had hoped and prayed it would not return, but I guess God had other plans in store for me. Not only had the tumor returned, but the doctor informed us that it was a jelly-like brain tumor and not a solid mass tumor.

If it had been a solid-mass tumor, they would have been able to get it all in one surgery. Since it was a jelly-like tumor, it would be next to impossible to completely remove it with one simple surgery and other methods of treatments would be necessary to shrink it. This jelly-like tumor meant it would be next to impossible to completely get rid of it. The doctor informed us that he thought it was possible to shrink it enough to allow me more time, but this would more than likely become an ongoing battle in my life. We agreed to do whatever was necessary to fight this thing and give me more time on this earth. I asked John to tell our girls about this devastating news and the upcoming surgery. I just couldn't bear to see their little faces when they found out.

This second surgery was more invasive than the first one, requiring my whole head to be shaved. Since it was more invasive and complicated than the first one, I came out of surgery with my left arm partially paralyzed, but they assured me that with physical and occupational therapy, I should regain some use of my left arm again.

Despite the setback with my arm, I had a pretty quick recovery. A year had passed after this surgery with no symptoms of any kind, and I was feeling hopeful again. I was trying to continue to stay involved in my girls' lives as much as possible and still trying to volunteer at our church as much as my body would allow. I was always a girly kind of girl wearing makeup, fixing my hair, making sure my purse and shoes matched my outfit, and making sure my nails were filed just right. So when I had my hair shaved after this second surgery, it was difficult for me to feel good about myself afterward. I wore headwraps until my hair started to grow back.

One day while driving down the highway during this time, John reached over the front seat of the car where I was sitting and grabbed my hand and started singing a song to me by a country music star named Randy Travis called "Forever and Ever, Amen" to make me feel better. It went like this:

"They say time take its toll on a body / makes a young girl's brown hair turn gray / Well, honey, I don't care, I ain't in love with your hair, and if it all fell out, I'd love you anyway / Darlin, I'm gonna love you forever / Forever and ever, amen."

John was always singing silly country songs, and believe it or not, he had a pretty decent singing voice. He would always cheer me up with a tune!

I was still able to drive at this point in life. We had an older vehicle which still had windows that you had to roll up and down by hand. Power windows were not in our budget in this stage of life. With the limited use of my left hand, sometimes operating the vehicle became a challenge. One of the girls would always sit up in front with me and help me hold the steering wheel or roll the window up and down for me if I needed help with my left hand. I know they liked to think they were helping me drive.

Unfortunately, just about a year and a half after this second surgery, a routine CT scan showed the tumor was once again back. This thing was not going away just as the doctor had told us. The neurosurgeon that I was seeing showed more concern this time and didn't want to do the same surgery as he had done in the previous surgery. He advised us to consider doing some experimental hyperthermia treatments to shrink the tumor. Hyperthermia treatments had not been around too long back in the 1980s. It was still an experimental procedure. These treatments would involve drilling several holes into the skull around the base of the tumor and placing probes into the holes where radiation heat would be applied to shrink the tumor. Since these treatments were still considered experimental, our medical insurance did not cover the cost of this.

We knew we had to try it though because I was in my early 30s and had two young daughters. I trusted my doctor, and if he said this is what we needed to try, I wanted to try it. I knew that God would take care of me, he had already shown me his faithfulness in the past, and I trusted in my faith!

I prayed and asked God to allow me to get through this one more time and to give me enough years and time left to see my girls grow up a little bit more.

My daily prayer became one like this: "Lord, I believe in you and know I am saved and going to heaven. I look forward to heaven and spending an eternity with you. When you say my time is up, I trust you. But if it would be your will, I would ask for a little more time to watch my girls, that you blessed me with, grow up some more."

Once I started these experimental hyperthermia treatments in January of 1987, my life was forever changed. During the treatments, the radiation that passed through the probes had to kill off some good cells in order to kill the bad cells that were growing. In doing so, after the very first treatment, I was left completely paralyzed on my left side. I did eventually come home, but this time, in a wheelchair.

John got to work immediately at home, making it safe for me to be in a wheelchair. One project included building a large ramp for me to get in and out of the main door since I was unable to go up and down stairs now. No longer was just my left arm partially dysfunctional, but my whole left side was gone, including the feeling in my left leg. The hospital sent out occupational and physical therapists to our home to follow up with me, and I continued therapy for several months after the treatment. I was eventually able to walk with the assistance of a cane and got some use of my leg but could never get my arm to cooperate. It just hung there limp and lifeless. Most of the time, I had to keep it wrapped up in a sling because if I didn't, my shoulder would dislocate and come of out the socket.

Almost every time we went back in for a routine CT scan, the tumor continued to show up again and again. I continued to pray the same prayer: "God, please allow me a little more time to watch my girls grow up."

Every birthday that rolled around on December 2, I would sing loudly with my sister at the end of the birthday song "and many more" because I truly wanted a few more years to see my girls grow up.

We continued to fight this brain tumor with more surgeries followed by hyperthermia radiation treatments. In a span of two years, I had nine hyperthermia radiation treatments. Consequently, after several of these treatments, the skin around my skull where the probes had been placed were starting to burn away, and I now needed a skin graft surgery to replace the damaged skin and tissue. Skin grafts are layers of skin taken from another part of the body. Most of my skin grafts were taken from the inner and outer parts of my thighs and the buttocks area.

I mentioned before that these treatments were "experimental" during the years I was receiving care. Therefore, our medical insurance was not paying for them. The medical bills were pouring in from the hospital. Our church family held a benefit for me where the whole community was invited and tried to raise as much money as possible to help us. The benefit was successful and did help a ton, but it was still not enough.

John had taken a lot of time off work to be with me during all the hospital stays, and he was trying to still raise and look after our girls. Needless to say, we were drowning in debt, leaving us backed up on our mortgage payments for our beautiful home we had built together. We often wondered when the bank would have "enough" of our late payments.

God did allow me a break from all the surgeries and treatments. Surprisingly, I was tumor free for two years after all these hyperthermia treatments. During these two years though, we had to make some dramatic changes. The hardest one was that we had to give our beautiful house back to the bank. We just couldn't afford the payments anymore with all the medical bills we had and all the time John had to take off work to help care for me.

We moved our family into a rental home closer to my parents. The rental payment on this house was half the cost of the monthly mortgage we had been paying. My parents, other family members, and friends were a huge blessing to us during this time. They helped in every way possible. Helping us move, taking care of me, all the packing, bringing us meals, and looking after the girls. I thanked God for them daily! It truly does matter who you surround yourself with living life. Without the support and help from my family and church family, I don't know how we would have made it through these tough times.

This transition was especially hard for the girls. They had to say goodbye to their school where they had been attending all their life and say goodbye to their childhood home. Life didn't seem fair and definitely was not going as I had planned or imagined years ago.

As we settled in and got the girls enrolled into their new schools, I remained steady in my faith that God would never leave me or forsake me because I believed his Word. Nothing happens to us that hasn't already passed through the hands of God first. I had to trust and believe that even when I couldn't understand what was happening around me, I had to just keep praying for the Lord to help me persevere and get through one day at a time. There was nothing else I could do but believe in the promise that God works all things together for our good.

Shortly after our move once again, the tumor returned. It was getting to the point that every time I went back to the doctor for a checkup and CT scan, I expected it. Once again, another surgery took place, followed by more radiation treatments. During this surgery, some very dramatic events took place for us. I almost passed away, and my life was in a dangerously critical condition.

John and my mother were waiting in the waiting room to hear news on my condition when the doctor rushed in to find John.

"We are losing Linda. Her vitals are fading quickly. John, I need your approval to rush her downstairs and put her into a hyperbaric chamber. If we don't, she will be gone within a few minutes."

"Yes, Doctor, do whatever is necessary to help her."

My skull and brain had been put through so much, it just didn't want to cooperate this time around. This hyperbaric oxygen chamber would pump 100 percent oxygen into my brain that was escaping from all the events of the recent surgery. The chamber would allow blood and oxygen to flow to my organs and brain at a greater rate versus normal atmospheric pressure.

John was allowed to go into the room where this chamber was and sit with me in a small waiting area. I have no recollection of getting into the chamber, but I do remember waking up inside of it for a brief time and not knowing where I was. I called out for someone to answer me, "Hello, where am I? What's happening?"

John spoke to me through a small speaker on the side of the chamber, "Linda, it's me, John. You are inside an oxygen chamber. I know it's scary but please don't be afraid. They are pumping oxygen into your body to help you recover from the surgery. I'm sitting right next to you, and I'll stay with you, please don't be afraid and just try to rest."

"John, please keep talking to me."

His voice was music to my soul and gave me the strength to relax and accept what was happening. I didn't talk back much as I faded in and out of consciousness.

I was in the intensive care unit in critical condition for several days after this ordeal hanging on for dear life. I was unconscious and unresponsive to the outside world coming in to see me during this time, but I was very much responsive in my spiritual realm, having deep conversations with the Lord.

For days, I laid in that recovery bed, dreaming about heaven and how beautiful it would be when I got there. I thought of all my family members that had passed on before me that I would get to see when I get there. I wasn't able to move my lips and say an out loud prayer, but God hears the cries of our soul and heart. I prayed for my girls during this time of recovery from the depths of my soul. I spoke to the Lord and told him I couldn't wait to get to heaven, and I was ready but asked if I could have just a few more years to watch my girls finish growing up.

My soul cried out for their safety and protection and that God would send wonderful people into their lives to look over them in my absence. I could feel that my time on this earth was limited. I had visions of heaven and felt as if I was in the Lord's presence the whole time while in that recovery period. I was a firm believer in the Bible and believed the verse from Revelation 21:4: "He will wipe away all tears from their eyes; and there shall be no more death, neither sorrow, nor crying, neither shall there be any more pain; for the old world and its evils are gone forever."

I was clinging tightly to that passage of scripture that all my pain, tears, and sorrows would vanish forever after one moment in the presence of the Almighty King when I entered heaven.

During this same time while I was in recovery in the ICU, my younger sister and her husband came to visit me. Karen Sue had been married for quite some time now. I was so blessed to have had the strength and energy to be a bridesmaid in her wedding and be able to walk down the aisle at their ceremony.

At the time of her wedding, I still had the use of my left leg. I did wear a wig during the wedding though because my natural hair was just not cooperating and growing back as fast as I had hoped. After several years of their marriage, they had desired to have children and to start a family. They had many disappointments and challenges with this though. Getting pregnant with their first child required the assistance of some infertility treatments.

When they finally had a successful treatment and found out they were expecting their first child, I was unconscious and laid up in the ICU bed. I was unresponsive and not communicating during this time. Karen reported to me from my bedside, "Linda, you're never going to believe the wonderful news we have. We're having a baby. I'm pregnant!"

I have no memory of her telling me this in the hospital. However, my family later reported to me when I came out of my state of unconsciousness that when Karen told me the good news, I had tears that ran down the side of my cheek. I could hear what my family was saying to me, I just couldn't respond to anything. My heart was so happy for my sister and her husband.

Several weeks after that surgery and finally recovering and coming back to a conscious state and just a few days before I was scheduled to go home, they found fluid building up in my skull. A shunt was now needed. The shunt was a tube surgically placed in the brain to help drain cerebrospinal fluid and redirect it to another location in the body where it can be reabsorbed. This shunt was placed to reduce the pressure and swelling on my brain from the reoccurring tumor and to reduce fluid buildup. That left me with more days spent in the hospital. I was so grateful for my mother, my sister, and our friends that took such good care of my girls during this time.

My sister, Karen Sue, turned out to not only be my birthday buddy, but one of my greatest blessings in life by helping me raise the girls. Because of her and my parents, my girls had everything they needed when I was physically unable to be there for them. I was able to endure all my hospital stays and operations, knowing they had everything under control with our girls.

Because I had so many surgeries and radiation treatments on my skull, I was left with a lot of skin and tissue damage. The doctor had to perform another surgery similar to that of a cranioplasty.

A cranioplasty is the surgical repair of the bone defect in the skull that's left behind after a previous operation or injury. A titanium plate was prefabricated and molded at the time of the surgery to custom fit the original skull piece that was cut away. After that, another skin graft surgery was also needed to make sure I looked somewhat cosmetically friendly.

This was a very risky surgery and left me with several complications and side effects.

Throughout all these numerous different surgeries, I developed several infections both inside and outside the skull. Upon one of the infections, it was necessary to open my skull back up and remove the plate and allow the tissue and skull to heal and then we had to replace it again. This was a very long and strenuous procedure and drained our family in every way possible. I was in and out of the hospital several times during the course of one year and stayed in a rehab section of the hospital for a few weeks while recovering. I was back in occupational and physical therapy to try to keep my strength up and regain the use of my left leg that had been paralyzed. Some days it seemed to want to cooperate, and other days, it just wouldn't do what I wanted.

After this plate surgery, skin graft, and the recovery that came along with this, I was once again back at home. Once I was home, I found myself in unfamiliar territory. I was on several different medications, and I was tired all the time. My left leg hindered my ability to get around, and I just couldn't get my body to function as I wanted to.

During this time, my bladder started to be uncooperative, and I began urinating on myself during naps and at bedtime and sometimes even just sitting around on the couch while watching TV. John and the girls were constantly cleaning up after me. We decided it was best to keep Depends underpants on me full-time. It was very discouraging for me mentally to realize what was happening to my body and to know that I was wearing "diapers."

Not even forty years old yet and I was a disabled, tired, wet mess wearing an adult diaper. I don't think you need me to explain what was going on in my marriage at this point in time. There really was not much of a marriage anymore. No fun outings or dates because it was just easier for me to stay home. John had become my caretaker, and it was taking a toll on him in a big way. Our financial situation was a mess. We were drowning in medical bills. The insurance company had dropped me off of the plan because I exceeded my limit with all the numerous surgeries and hospital stays. John couldn't find an insurance company to cover me with all my medical conditions. He was under a tremendous amount of stress.

This was by far one of the hardest years of my life. John left early each morning to go to work, and the girls would get up early each school day to help care for me before leaving for school. The girls were twelve and sixteen at this point, and they were basically my caretakers, taking care of all of the needs of the house too. If they wanted clean laundry, a home cooked meal, or anything else for that matter, they had to tend to it themselves, or it just didn't get done.

John was so good to teach the girls how to cook good meals for us. We had spaghetti and pancakes a lot because that was very quick and easy for them. I would sit on the couch in the living room and watch my youngest daughter stand next to her dad at the stove and listen to him teach her when to watch the batter bubble up on the pancake mix to know when to flip them at the right time. I was so thankful for his guidance and help to teach them necessary life skills. I wanted to teach my girls a lot of things, but I just couldn't find any motivation or strength with all my prescription medications.

The medications made me very tired, and I slept a lot. John and the girls had to help me back and forth to the bathroom because after a trip by myself one day, I found myself face first in the bathtub because my left leg failed me. I had to take a shower sitting on a bath stool inside the tub because I couldn't stand for that long with my weak leg.

John or one of the girls had to help me every time I needed in or out of the shower to make sure I didn't have any more falls. I felt so helpless, and I prayed constantly all the time that God would give us the strength we needed to endure this hard season of life. I didn't want to continue to live like this, but I continued to pray and ask God for a few more years to just see my girls grow up into young women. All I wanted was to watch them grow up. They were so beautiful and precious to me, I just couldn't leave them yet.

Chapter 7

The Divorce

You may never know that JESUS is all
you need, until JESUS is all you have.
—Corrie Ten Boom

Raising a family and keeping love alive in a marriage with a spouse who is constantly sick, in constant pain, or living with a disability is an extreme challenge. The divorce rate in couples with a disability or a severe chronic medical condition hovers around 90 percent, and when you add financial pressure on top of that, sometimes "love" can't keep you together anymore.

Our marriage was falling apart. John barely came home anymore, we didn't talk about anything other than necessary medical treatment for me. He had taken on the role as my caretaker, and we had not been intimate in a very long time. My role as a loving wife had vanished into thin air, and I felt John slipping away. I knew hard times were coming. I could feel it in my spirit. I often worried about him. I worried that this was more than he could handle. I prayed for him that he would not suffer from a mental or nervous breakdown. I prayed that he would stay healthy. I was not able to offer much to my family at this point in life, but one thing I could do was pray, so pray is what I did!

John's absence from the home got longer and longer until I knew one day he was not returning.

My oldest daughter was sixteen years old at this time, and one afternoon when she was leaving for work, she found a note in the front seat of her car with an envelope of money. The note read this:

> Shug, I am very sorry, but Dad will not be coming home tonight or anytime soon. I need some space to think. This money will cover a month's worth of medications to care for your mom. I will be in touch with you soon.

My daughter brought the note into the house and showed me. What should have been a huge disappointment and shock to me really wasn't. I know the Lord prepared my spirit for this day. The Lord had been so faithful to me in every area of my life in the past. I knew he would never leave me or forsake me. I knew he was working all things together for my good, even now in a time when I felt like I was walking through the valley of death.

> *The Lord is my shepherd, I shall not want. He maketh me to lie down in green pastures, he leadeth me beside the still waters. He restores my soul. Yea, though I walk through the valley of the shadow of death, I will fear no evil, for thou art with me, thy rod and thy staff they comfort me.* (Psalm 23, KJV)

Psalm 23 carried me through the pain and sadness I was feeling. Yes, I cried and had my emotional days, realizing that my marriage, my love story to John was over, but what a wonderful love story it had been. Most people never find true love like what I had with John years ago, and I was so grateful for the wonderful memories with which I was blessed. I was grateful for the blessing of daughters that the marriage had brought us, and I hoped and prayed that my girls wouldn't remember this horrible part of the end of our story, but all the good parts from the good years before this sickness and disability took over my life.

What I wanted my girls to remember the most during this most difficult time in our life was the fact that life is hard…*but God is good*!

People are always going to fail us whether it's a spouse, a child, a parent, a friend, or another family member. God didn't intend for other people to be our saviors. He is the only one that can fulfill our inner most desires and give us everything we need inside. His word says in the book of Deuteronomy that he will never leave us or forsake us.

Shortly after we found John's note in my daughter's car, we began to make plans to move into my parents' home which was just a few short minutes away in the same town. The girls didn't have to switch schools again, so it wasn't too much change for them. Moving in with my parents was probably one of the best things that could have happened for me and the girls. My sweet mother jumped right in and finished raising the girls as her own. What I could no longer do, she was right there to help.

As we said goodbye to another chapter in life, we pressed right on forward with whatever God had in store for us now. John and I did get divorced. I was apprehensive when I first received the divorce papers and wanted to contest it. But after much prayer and thought, I knew it was the right thing to do. Our marriage had suffered a tremendous amount of stress and damage, and I knew I was in no condition to be a loving wife to him anymore. I signed the papers and prayed for his happiness and health and that he could move on with his life.

The divorce was very hard on all of us, especially on my youngest daughter as she just didn't understand what was happening to our family. I prayed all the time that God would show her his grace, mercy, and forgiveness over time. Through all the hardships that life was throwing our way, I knew I had to remain positive and not complain. How could I dare complain about life when the Bible tells us clearly in the book of Job chapter 14 that God determines our days.

"How frail is humanity! How short life is, and how full of trouble! Like a flower, we blossom for a moment and then wither. Like the shadow of a passing cloud, we quickly disappear. Must you keep an eye on such a frail creature and demand an accounting from me? Who can create purity in one born impure? No one! You O Lord have decided the length of our lives. You know how many months we will live, and we are not given a minute longer."

I believed with all my heart that nothing comes to us that hasn't already passed through the hands of God first. If I believed that, I had to live it out. I decided one day while in my bedroom, living in my parents' home that for the remainder of my days, I would show the world around me by my attitude and actions, that if God is for me, who can be against me? My prayer was that my friends, family, and all other acquaintances would know I was not going to let this tragedy of a failed marriage and poor health destroy me but rather strengthen my faith and belief in an Almighty God.

Sometimes it was very hard for me and my friends and family to deal with the hard question of "Why wasn't God healing me?" We prayed and prayed for physical healing for this brain tumor to go away, and for me to have a perfect physical healing. We may never get the luxury while living here on earth of knowing the "why" all the time to life's hard questions. I believe when we get on the other side of heaven and enter his presence, we will get all our answers, and it will be all that we need. Until then, we just have to keep trusting that his ways are so much higher than our ways.

> *"For I know the plans I have for you, says the Lord. They are plans for good and not for disaster, to give you a future and a hope"* (Jeremiah 29:11, NLT).

Chapter 8

The Knot

Because of God's tender mercy, the light from
heaven is about to break upon us, to give light
to those who sit in darkness and in the shadow
of death, and to guide us to the path of peace.
—Luke 1:78–79 (NLT)

I was surprisingly getting stronger each day in my left side where I had been so weak before. Enough so that I ventured out on a shopping trip with my mother and my youngest daughter one afternoon. I didn't have a lot of hair at the time because I kept it very short, but it was growing back very nicely this time around. Every time I went in for surgery, they would shave it, so I just kept it very short and most of the time would just wear headwraps. I wore headwraps mostly because I needed to cover up all the scars on my skull and head from all the surgeries.

The hair never grew back in the places where I had the holes drilled from the hyperthermia treatments. I tried several different wigs, but they were always so hot and itchy, I just preferred the headwraps. I was not wearing a headwrap or a wig, just my natural hair this day since it had decided to grow a little more than normal. It was quite windy on this particular day.

My mother pushed my wheelchair up next to the car, so I could transfer into it. And while we were making the transfer, the wind blew my hair back in such a way that she noticed a huge knot on the side of my skull just above where all my previous surgeries were. She sat me back down in the car and told me to look in the mirror and asked me if I had noticed this knot before or not. Honestly, I had not taken notice to it. I didn't pay much attention to myself anymore. Most of the time, I preferred to not look at that section of myself because of all the scars and damage that had been done. We decided I better make a doctor's appointment to have this checked out.

Sure enough, the tumor was back once again. And this time, pressing outward from the skull, hence the knot on my forehead. Every time the tumor grew back, it had grown out to another part of the brain and different treatments were necessary to shrink it.

Another surgery was performed, and this time followed up by both radiation and some chemotherapy treatments. These treatments really did me in, and the chemotherapy made me very sick. My mom and the girls were constantly taking care of me and making sure I had everything I needed whenever the chemo made me sick. I now had a portable bedside commode (toilet) in my bedroom next to the bed because it was easier for the family to just let me go to the bathroom in there than walk me down the hallway.

I hardly ever left my bedroom anymore. In-home nurses from the hospital would visit me weekly to check the status of my recovery and make sure I had everything I needed. My meals were brought to me in the bedroom. The room was big enough for a small loveseat sofa and a small TV entertainment center, and I just watched TV and worked crossword and word search puzzles all day to try and keep my mind active.

My youngest daughter would come in my bedroom after a day at school and spend time with me. We would watch TV together, play scrabble, and just catch up on what was going on in her life. My oldest daughter was in her senior year of high school and working a lot of hours to make money, so my time with her was very limited as she was busy developing into a wonderful young lady.

I had spent so much time in the hospital over the years, including some holidays, that the girls missed out on a lot of their childhood. They spent days and nights camping out in the waiting room of the neurosurgery department of the hospital. My mom would bring in their sleeping bags and pillows, board games, books, and playing cards to keep them occupied during all the long waiting time. Thankfully there was television and vending machines in the waiting area too that helped pass the time. My family would take turns during all the recovery periods of all my numerous surgeries and visit with me. Usually only two people at a time could come in to see me. My parents and the girls were so faithful to sit and wait at the hospital. They didn't want to leave me because I was always in such critical condition during the recovery periods.

During one of my surgeries and radiation treatments, it was near Christmas time. The hospital had a holiday project called "The Giving Angel Tree." This project picked out a special family in need during the holidays and blessed them with gifts. My girls were picked that year, and they were showered with Christmas gifts from the hospital. After coming home from a recent treatment, my mother answered a knock on the front door. And when she opened the door, there were two nurses from the hospital that we were very familiar with (having spent so much time there) holding bags of presents for my two girls.

What a blessing and joy this brought to all of us. We were so thankful for God's blessings to us during that Christmas season and for looking out for us. When the holidays are upon us and circumstances seem so discouraging, God is always sending little reminders of hope that he is always looking out for us and taking care of us.

At this point in my life, I was now forty-two years old. The girls were sixteen and twenty. My oldest daughter was in college and working part-time. She lived on her own in a rental home with a friend. She was doing so well, and I was very proud of her. My youngest daughter just started her very first job at a pizza joint in town, and my mother taught her how to drive and had just helped her get her driver's license. I was so thankful for all my mother's support and care for us when I could not do what I wanted to do. She stepped in and picked up the pieces where I could not.

From the beginning of this crisis, we all prayed for my physical healing, but my biggest prayer was that I could fight this tumor long enough to watch my girls grow up. All I ever wanted during this ordeal was enough time to see them grow up into young women and see that they could take care of themselves.

I was fortunate to have found true love with a man early in life, but what I didn't know was that at the end of my life, I really discovered "true love" with the one that created me in his own image.

In Genesis, the Bible tells us that God created man in his own image. He created them male and female. When my spouse chose to leave our marriage, I didn't let another person's choices destroy me. I used it as a stepping stone to draw closer to God. I had a lot of extra time on my hands in my little bedroom in my parents' home to pray and spend time with the Lord. In doing that, I found my ultimate one true love—my Savior, my Friend, Jesus!

"So God created people in his own image; God patterned them after himself; male and female he created them" (Genesis 1:27, NLT).

Chapter 9

Inoperable

*My home is in Heaven, I'm just
traveling through this world.*
—Billy Graham

I was now going in every six months for a checkup and CT scan of
my brain, and I hadn't had a positive checkup appointment in years
now. Every time I went in, there was something I needed treatment
or surgery for. The doctor called my mother at home one morning
and reported he needed us to come in to his office to discuss the
results of the most recent CT scan.

"Linda, the tumor is back, and I've never seen it like this before.
It has spread in a new direction. After much thought and counsel
with other physicians, I am so sorry to tell you, but we will not be
able to operate on this tumor anymore, and there is nothing else I
can do for you to fight this." The doctor went on to tell me that I
had approximately nine months to live, and it was in my best interest to entertain the idea of putting me into a nursing home facility
within the next few months as my body and organs would begin to
shut down completely from the tumor. I would need twenty-four-
hour full-time care in the next few months as the tumor continued
to grow.

At a moment when I should have been beside myself with fear and worry about the thought of death, it was the opposite. I had such peace and confidence because I knew where my next home would be…*heaven*!

My response to the doctor was this: "My prayer and desire has always been for a few more years to fight this tumor so I could watch my girls grow up, and you have helped me do that. I have lived a good life, and I'm ready to go home."

Over the course of all my surgeries and treatments, my doctor was constantly amazed at my recovery and how they were always able to successfully shrink the tumor when it really seemed medically impossible. I developed a deep friendship with my neurosurgeon and his staff, and he would always say before I went in for a surgery or a treatment that he would do all that he could to help me get those few more years I was longing for to be with my girls.

I truly believed that God was guiding the doctor's hands and watching over me during every surgery and procedure. I was truly thankful for a devoted medical professional that was always exploring new treatments and ideas to help me fight this tumor.

With that final doctor visit, we went back to my parents' home and started to make plans for the end of my life. The news was devastating to our friends and family, but I did my best to remain strong and confident. My youngest daughter (age sixteen) took the news the hardest. She cried a lot and hung out in my bedroom with me for days after the news and would sit on the loveseat sofa with me for hours and watch TV with me. I would tell her how proud I was of her and that I wanted her to continue living a good life and graduate high school and get a good job.

Alone with my thoughts, I would often dream about all that I would miss out on. Their weddings, their children, their futures. I wasn't about to complain though because I was grateful the Lord granted me my one prayer to watch them grow up into beautiful young ladies. I knew they could make it without me now. Everything was falling into place, and I could feel it was time for me to let go.

Chapter 10

The Nursing Home

*Trust in the Lord with all your heart
and lean not on your own understanding; in all your ways acknowledge him,
and he will make your paths straight.*
—Proverbs 3:5 (NIV)

My mother's sister, Aunt Emmagene, and her husband, Carlos, owned and operated a nursing home facility in the same state where we lived. This facility was about two hours away from my parents' residence though. When my mother broke the news to her, they both agreed that I should come and stay with them since I needed to be in a nursing home. It was heartbreaking for my mother to have to consider putting me into a home, so if she had to make this choice, having me with her sister was the best choice.

We packed my things up and made the journey to my aunt's hometown. It was a day filled with tears and sadness as my family got me settled in and started to make their way back home without me. My youngest daughter and mother had become my daily care-givers, and it was very hard on them to leave me in the home. They got my room in the home all neatly decorated and made sure I had everything I needed before they left. My mother left with confidence that her sister would see that her nursing staff would take excellent care of me.

God is always working in mysterious ways behind the scenes when we have no idea why he does things. Several years before my divorce and moving in with my parents, one of my dearest friends, Patty, moved away. She had been a huge blessing to me in my early years of sickness and treatment. Always helping to care for my girls when they needed to spend the night somewhere. Helping me around the house and even cooking meals for us. She was a great listener, friend, and prayer partner. I was very saddened when she and her husband announced they were moving away to another town.

Little did I know, but this new town where her family moved to was now just fifteen short miles away from the nursing home where I was now residing. When Patty found out I was staying in my aunt's facility, she would visit me weekly with encouragement and prayers. While staying at the nursing home, my favorite day of the week became Sunday.

Patty and her husband would pick me up and drive me to her home church, so I could get out of the nursing home for a few hours. During the praise and worship music at the beginning of the service, Patty would help me walk down the center aisle of their church for prayer every time I went with them. It took me a long time to walk anywhere because I had to use a cane and have assistance on the other side by someone holding me. My left leg never fully regained the strength from the surgery that paralyzed it.

I walked down to the front of that church every time I visited with a smile on my face, eagerly wanting the pastor to pray over me for God's will to be done. I wasn't sure what to pray for anymore. I just knew I had to trust, believe, and pray through no matter what the outcome.

The highlight before heading back to my room at the nursing home was that we would stop at the local Steak n' Shake where I would order a steak burger, french fries, and my favorite milkshake.

What a blessing this dear friend was to me! Years ago, when I thought God had taken one of my dearest friends away from me, he was actually moving her to a place to be a blessing to me down the road when I would need it the most.

My girls would drive down and visit me once a month and stay for a whole day on a Saturday. I was always so glad when they came down to see me. It felt good to know my girls were able to be on their own now, making my exit from this earthly life easier to cope with. I knew that my God would see to all their needs.

Chapter 11

The Finish Line

I have fought the good fight, I have finished the race, I have kept the faith. Finally, there is laid up for me the crown of righteousness, which the Lord, the righteous Judge will give to me on that day. The prize is not just for me but for all who eagerly look forward to his glorious return.
—2 Timothy 4:7–8 (NIV)

After about six months at my aunt's facility, the tumor started to push outward of my skull, and a huge knot was growing on the right side of my forehead. It was red and warm, and we knew the tumor was now progressing. I was tired all the time, slept a lot, and I was starting to show signs of dementia.

My Sunday outings with my friend, Patty, had to stop because I was not getting around well at all anymore. Just as the doctor had said, my organs were starting to slow down from the tumor.

My mother began to feel the strain of my ailing health and was no longer satisfied with me being so far away from her and the girls. She knew my time of death was nearing and wanted me to be closer to them. She began to look into nursing home facilities closer to their home. I was moved into a new nursing home just a few short miles from my parents' home right before my forty-third birthday. I had just been there a few short weeks, and the nursing staff allowed my parents and family to have a big birthday party for me in the dining hall after dinner hours one evening. We all knew this would be my last birthday to celebrate, so they went all out!

My friends and family were all there. Balloons, music, cake, and punch for all. I was delighted to be surrounded by everyone that I loved. My youngest daughter would be seventeen years old in just a few weeks. When she arrived at my birthday party, she brought a handsome young man with her. I had never seen him before and was anxious to meet him. I wasn't talking very well and couldn't carry on a conversation much and was now in a roll-around bed full-time and on a liquid puree diet. My daughter had brought her new boyfriend with her, and this was our first time to meet. She introduced this young man to me, and I was so pleased she had met a nice young gentleman.

I was so delighted to see both of my girls in such a good place in their lives. I was thankful for the friends and family that I knew would continue to give them the support they would need in the next few months and even years as we said goodbye. Little did I know that day, but I got to meet my daughter's future husband at that final birthday party. They were married three years later. I would say that the Lord had richly blessed my prayer request to see my girls grow up because he continued to show me favor in every way possible.

Just three short months after my fabulous birthday bash, my health went downhill fast. All of my organs started to fail me from the pressure on my brain from the tumor. My mind deteriorated, and I talked like a young child and spoke about memories from my childhood when I was in grade school. Sometimes I didn't recall my family when they came to visit me. It was much like a state of dementia. My thoughts were very confused, and I talked very silly. I no longer got up out of my bed and began to develop extremely bad bedsores. Some of them were infected, and the infections were not good for my health. My respiratory system was not functioning well, and I constantly had trouble breathing and was on full-time oxygen.

Toward the end of my life, my mother and youngest daughter who was still residing in her care, would go to sleep at night with their regular clothes on because they knew they could get a call at any minute that my life was nearing the end.

On the final day of my life here on earth, my family was called in to the nursing home about 2:00 a.m. My mother and youngest daughter arrived first at my bedside as the family was all called in to say their final goodbyes.

My daughter crawled up in the bed with me and laid with me for about an hour before all the others arrived and laid her head in my neck and sang some of my favorite gospel hymns to me. Songs about heaven and the goodness of the Lord.

As my pastor and family members arrived in my room that early morning, my blood pressure began to drop to a very dangerous level, and I was no longer able to breathe on my own anymore. As my life began to fade from this earthly home, I was surrounded by all my beloved immediate family members and my pastor from my home church. They sang heavenly gospel hymns to me around my bedside and sang me to heaven as I breathed my final breathe here on earth.

Earth has no sorrow that heaven cannot heal...

Epilogue

*You did not choose me, but I choose you and
appointed you so that you might go and bear
fruit, fruit that will last and so that whatever
you ask in my name the Father will give you.*
                                   —John 15:16 (NIV)

When the death of a loved one comes upon you and leaves you with such grief and sadness, you can begin to wonder where God is in such circumstances. The Lord can use our darkest moments to totally change our perspective for our future.

When people ask me how I know God is real, this experience of my mother dying is my answer! The presence of God was so strong in the room the morning that my mother passed away. It was almost as if heavenly angels themselves swooped down and took my momma out of that bed and carried her away to heaven.

As we were singing her to heaven, a presence and light illuminated the room. It was an experience I will never forget. In my darkest moment, saying goodbye to my mother, God was working on my behalf to touch the lives of those left behind. He loved me so much; he left me with an experience I will never forget. An experience that gives me hope. A hope that there is so much more after we leave this earth.

As a grown woman now with a family of my own and having to deal with the daily challenges of life, I know that no matter what comes my way, I have an eternal hope of heaven.

Heaven is not a mythical place. It is the holy dwelling of the Lord Most High. And although we cannot even begin to comprehend its splendor, the Bible gives us beautiful descriptions of the place in which those who have received Jesus will spend their eternity.

> *That is why we never give up. Though our bodies are dying, our spirits are being renewed every day. For our present troubles are quite small and won't last very long. Yet they produce for us an immeasurably great glory that will last forever! So we don't look at the troubles we can see right now; rather, we look forward to what we have not yet seen. For the troubles we see will soon be over, but the joys to come will last forever.* (2 Corinthians 4:16–18, NLT)

Losing my mother at an early age and watching her endure all of life's challenges, has encouraged me to be a better mother to my sons. I am not promised tomorrow, so I have to make the days given to me matter.

As a mother to three sons, I can be quick to mutter, complain, show impatience, and raise my voice. I am reminded that my children are watching me and the way I handle life. Do I want them to see their mother leaving a legacy of anger, loud voices, impatience, and lack of self-control…or do I want them to witness love, forgiveness, patience, and kindness?

When life gets busy and hectic raising three boys, I can be quick to grumble about all I have to do and become irritated at the to-do list before me. It's in these moments, I remind myself that I get to do all these things on a to-do list.

My ability to get to do things with my children could be taken from me at any moment. My health and my circumstances could all change tomorrow. I'm sure my mother would have loved to have been able to run to ball games, practices, and the local department store multiple times in one day, but her situation would not allow her to do so. When life with kids starts to weigh heavily on me, I am reminded of my mother's legacy. I get to do all these things today— thank you, God, that I am blessed with good health to do things for my family today.

When challenges come my way, I want to strive to leave a legacy as my mother did. A legacy of endurance. A legacy of love. A legacy of forgiveness. A legacy of God-honoring faith. A legacy that people will remember of how good God is, even when our circumstances are not so good.

When something difficult or tragic happens to us, we can be quick to ask "where is God in all this?"

I prayed for my mom's physical healing for several years. I prayed for my family to not fall apart and for my parents to not get divorced. When our family was told she had 9 months to live, I prayed and even fasted from food for several days that she wouldn't die. I was praying. I was asking. I was just a kid believing in the power of prayer and living out what my mom had always taught me, which was when you don't know what to do, you just pray and ask.

I still can't tell you why God didn't answer my prayers for healing for my mom, but I can tell you that by faith I now understand that even when we don't understand, God is always working behind the scenes for the good of those that love him and serve him. God didn't answer my prayers for physical healing for her, but he did give me the strength my whole childhood to endure such hard times. Hard times that a kid shouldn't have to go through. He got me through a terrible hard time for many long years. There was a time when I would ask the hard questions such as "God, why did you allow this to happen to my mom and allow her to die and allow my family to be broken apart from this?" However, I don't ask that question anymore, and in fact, after everything has been said and done, I am truly thankful for what I have lived through and experienced because it has made me a much better person.

Because of Her… I have compassion for others that are hurting and going through difficult situations.

Because of Her… I have an inner strength that I would have never found on my own if I hadn't walked through what I have been through.

Because of Her… I know that when all feels broken, lost, sad and hopeless, I can look up and remember who my source is and know that I do have an eternal hope in Jesus my savior.

Because of Her… I know that Jesus is the ultimate healer of a broken heart and can heal internal wounds that human man can never heal.

Because of Her… Jesus, my Heavenly Father, has taken what Satan meant for harm in my life and worked it all out together for HIS good and I am a better person because of what I've been through. I am a better, stronger person because of what I've walked through with this story and no matter what you have walked through – you can be too if you will let HIM help you.

Because of Her

No life is without worth,
whatever the length.
While being formed,
our destiny is distinct.
Linda was no different; God is no respecter.
Though her years on earth were shortened,
She was truly a messenger.
Linda's life touched so many,
Bringing her gifts to all.
She did not realize just how many,
But there are plenty we can recall.
Her first appearance as a beautiful babe,
Brought joy to Mom and Dad.
They had a daughter to love and direct,
Because of her, their hearts were made glad.
On her ninth birthday, she got a surprise,
A baby was born in the night.
Assuming her role as a big sister,
Brought Linda much delight.
Then came a wedding and starting a home,
And two girls of her own to cherish.
The girls made life complete,
What more could anyone wish.
She was faithful to God, giving herself,
in service as a Missionette leader.

Because she loved, taught, and gave,
Young lives were touched by the Redeemer.
When tragedy struck, and she became sick,
It was evident her friends were many.
Support was provided, encouragement given,
For her recovery, they all did plea.
Good news, and bad over the years,
Brought emotional fluctuation.
But never did she throw in the towel,
Her race, she continued to run.
"I never thought this would happen to me,"
She said from her hospital bed.
But when we sang "happy birthday to you,"
She sang, "And many, many more ahead."
We have no answers to why the loss,
of this mother, daughter, and friend.
Relatives mourn, children grieve,
And wonder if they will mend.
What was her destiny, her purpose in life?
How has she made a mark?
Ask her parents how she gave them love,
And left in their heart a spark.
Or ask her sister, daughters, or friends,
Or ask the children she helped find the Lord.
Ask her pastor, neighbors, and nurses,
Their words will reveal the record.
Because of her, people were changed,
Hearts blended together in love,
Realizing the ultimate healing for all,
Will come when we all meet above.

Poem by Sara Snodgrass

In loving memory of

Linda Faye Hollmann (Brewer)

December 2, 1952–March 27, 1996

I was the social service director at Cedars Healthcare Center, where Linda Hollmann was a resident. She was much younger than most of the elderly residents there. I remember how beautiful she was, even with the large tumor that bumped out from her forehead. Her skin was clear and she had these wonderful, twinkly eyes. She was kind to everyone who attended her needs. In December of 1995, we had a birthday celebration in the cafeteria for all the residents who had birthdays that month. We had a big cake and the staff was busy making sure everyone had a piece. Unfortunately, Linda couldn't eat solid food at this point, but it was HER birthday month, so she was lined up at the front with the other honerees. Her food restriction didn't seem to matter to one of the patients there with Alzheimer's disease; I caught him on the side of Linda, feeding her his cake and she was gobbling that cake down as fast as he would spoon it into her mouth! By the time we got to them, she had pretty much finished it. She was fine and it did not cause any problems for her, thank God. I will never forget how much she enjoyed that moment, and I think of sweet Linda Hollmann whenever cake is offered to me.

Memory written by:
Michelle Reynolds-Gray

If you have never asked Jesus into your heart and would like to make sure you make it into Heaven when your time on this earth is over, please say this prayer out loud:

> "Father, I know that I am a sinner and that my sins separate me from you. I am truly sorry, and I want to run away from the sins in my past and follow you and your plan for my life. Please forgive me and help me turn away from sinful ways. I do believe that your son, Jesus died for my sins, was resurrected from the dead, is alive, and hears my prayer today. I invite you Jesus to become the Lord of my life and rule in my heart from this day forward. Please send your Holy Spirit to help me obey you and do your will for the rest of my life. In Jesus' name I pray, Amen."

If you said a sinner's prayer today, I personally want to welcome you into the family of God and encourage you to find a local home church to attend on a regular basis to spend time in worship. I would also love to hear from you and help you in anyway on your new journey with Jesus.

> *"If you declare with your mouth that Jesus*
> *is Lord and believe in your heart that*
> *God raised him from the dead, you will be saved."*
> *Romans 10:9 (NIV)*

About the Author

Amanda Schnable is a wife and mother to three boys. She lives in a small rural community in Fredericktown, Missouri, and writes from her kitchen table in her house in the woods. She enjoys spending time with her family and friends, volunteering at her church, cooking, baking, hiking, and spending time outdoors.

She works part-time at a dental office as a dental hygienist, but her favorite job is just simply being a wife, a mother, and friend to many. There is nothing she enjoys more than praying with women and helping them find a deeper connection with the Lord and finding beauty out of their ashes.

If you would like to connect with Amanda or have her speak at your church or women's conference,

She can be contacted at:
becauseofherthebook@gmail.com
Facebook page Because of Her

CPSIA information can be obtained
at www.ICGtesting.com
Printed in the USA
FFHW020600220819
54371667-60090FF

9 781644 926796